A
Healin... ...ps

...y
Paul Glen

Healing Client Relationships

A Professional's Guide to Managing Client Conflict

Paul Glen

Professional Service Publishing
Marina Del Rey, CA

Healing Client Relationships

A Professional's Guide to Managing Client Conflict

Paul Glen

Professional Service Publishing,
Marina Del Rey, CA

Healing Client Relationships: A Professional's Guide to Managing Client Conflict © 2001 Paul Glen

This book is copyrighted material. All rights are reserved.

Printed in the United States of America

Published by Professional Service Publishing
17 Northstar Street, Suite 202
Marina Del Rey, CA 90292
Toll Free: 877-814-7753, Fax: 310-745-1980

ISBN 0-9712468-0-7

This book is designed to provide information about the subject matter covered. Every effort has been made to make this book as complete and accurate as possible. It is sold with the understanding that the publisher and author are not engaged in rendering legal or financial advice. If legal or other expert assistance is required, the services of a competent professional should be sought.

The purpose of this book is to educate and entertain. The author and Professional Service Publishing shall have neither liability nor responsibility to any person or entity with respect to any loss or damage caused, or alleged to be caused, directly or indirectly, by the information contained in this book.

Any person not wishing to be bound by the above may return this book to the publisher for a refund.

Table of Contents

1. Introduction

If you are a professional and haven't yet experienced a broken client relationship, you are either young or lucky. No matter how brilliant, talented, and charismatic you are, eventually an angry, hurt or dissatisfied client will confront you.

How well you handle such situations governs, in many respects, the trajectory of your career. If you cannot heal damaged client relationships, you will be doomed to a career marked by short-term contracts, rare promotions and mediocre profitability. You will not be nearly as successful as those who handle client conflict well.

Healing client relationships is one of four key relationship management skills for professionals. If you can master all four in addition to the technology of your profession, you will be very successful. The full list includes:

- Establishing client relationships
- Managing client relationships
- Healing client relationships
- Selling follow-on work

This brief guide will help you excel in this critical area of client service. If you are new to managing client relationships, this guide will give you immediately applicable ideas to

jumpstart your abilities.   If you are more
seasoned, it will challenge you to continue to
develop your abilities.

Paul Glen
Marina Del Rey, CA

2.Unhappy Clients

2.1. Professionals and Unhappy Clients

As professionals, facing unhappy clients is one of the most difficult things that we do. Ordinarily, getting a call from a client is a pleasure. They want to seek our advice on issues of importance and to thank us for our valuable contributions to their businesses and lives. Sometimes they even want to buy more services.

No matter how competent, capable, and charismatic you are, at some point a client will be unhappy with you. You'll be surprised in a meeting. The phone will ring. Or you'll hear it through the grapevine. One of your clients is really upset with you.

How you handle that situation will determine whether you retain that relationship or lose the client.

Handling unhappy clients is particularly difficult for professionals. We identify with our work. It's an expression of self. We pride ourselves on its quality. When a client is unhappy with our work, we feel that they are unhappy with us personally and we tend to feel threatened.

Customer service representatives for the phone company don't have this problem. For them, detachment is easy. They know that the irate caller isn't angry with them personally, just at the vague distant monolith.

For professionals, irate clients threaten more than just personal comfort. They affect current and future financial stability by endangering the reputations that are built on happy clients. No single factor is more important to future sales.

Building a successful professional practice requires developing the skills to heal client relationships.

2.2. What Makes Clients Unhappy

Clients have high expectations regarding their professional relationships. When a client hires you, they have certain expectations about the results of your work together and the nature of your relationship. When you violate any of these, they may become disappointed, dissatisfied, or disillusioned.

Here's a short list of client expectations that are easy to violate. Generally, clients want:

- Respectful treatment
- Prompt responses
- Coherent explanations which *they* can understand
- Competent service
- Choices which they can make about their future
- Undivided attention
- Dedicated service
- Updates on progress and problems
- Confidence in your trustworthiness

And only lastly:

- Excellent technical work

As professionals, we are captivated by the quality of our work and often fool ourselves into believing that this is the most important thing to clients just because it's the most important thing to us. It's not. In fact, clients rarely know if your specialist, technical work is outstanding.

If a client knew enough about your specialty to distinguish outstanding technical work, they wouldn't need to hire you.

Clients rarely know if your technical work is outstanding.

2.3. The Cost of Losing Clients

It's been well documented that the cost of acquiring new clients greatly exceeds the cost of retaining clients. Selling work to someone who knows and trusts you is much easier than selling to someone who doesn't.

Why?

Simple. When selling professional services, you have only one thing to offer...TRUST. Think about it. Whether you're a consultant, lawyer, accountant, or other professional, the sales process is essentially the same. You discuss the client's problem and offer a service that will hopefully solve the customer's problem. To the client, they are always paying for a service that they can't try out, sample, or review. They're just stuck paying and hoping.

Once you've worked with a client and they are satisfied, they are much more likely to trust you with more work rather than go out and try to find another professional who is completely unknown.

So once you've established a relationship, losing that client costs you a lot more than just the fees from that one project. For most professionals, repeat business is their bread and butter. When you lose a client, you lose:

- Future business from that client
- Business from those they would have referred to you
- Business from those they tell about their unhappiness

In short, handling client complaints well determines, in part, how successfully you grow your practice.

When selling professional services, you have only one thing to offer...TRUST.

3. What To Do

In this section, you will be introduced to the Relationship Healing Process, an 8-step approach to productively resolve client conflict.

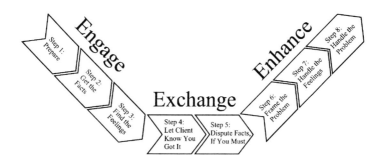

3.1. Step 1: Be Prepared

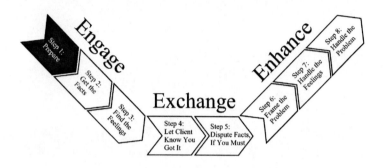

Usually, client unhappiness comes as a surprise. In fact, in my experience, it seems to show up most often when you are particularly proud of your work. Just when you think that the client will appreciate your brilliance, the client complains. There are occasional cases when you can anticipate some sort of concern, such as when you miss a delivery deadline or a project has run over budget. But, most of the time, you don't see it coming.

Your effectiveness at the moment of crisis will govern how difficult it will be to retain the client relationship. If you handle the first encounter poorly, it will be much more difficult to heal the relationship than if you handle it well.

That's why you need to be constantly prepared for client concerns.

There are two ways to prepare:

Know the project and the environment. If you stay on top of the status of client projects, you will foresee many of the likely sources of dissatisfaction. Knowing what is going on in the rest of the client's environment also helps you anticipate problems. For example, if you are working on a marketing campaign with a customer and discover that one of their competitors has beaten them to the punch, you can expect the client to be frustrated and perhaps dissatisfied with the speed of the project.

Know the client culture. If the members of the client's organizational culture exhibit blaming behaviors, expect more problems. If the individual client you are serving has a negative outlook, steel yourself.

3.1.1. Prepare Yourself

You must prepare yourself emotionally for client conflict as well as intellectually. If you have the luxury of a warning that the problem is coming, take a little time to put yourself in the right frame of mind to heal the relationship. Whatever your comfort level with conflict, it will help you to be prepared.

For those of you to whom confrontation is quite comfortable (e.g. trial attorneys), it's important to realize that your clients may not be as comfortable as you are and you will need to prepare yourself to tone down your natural responses.

For those of you to whom confrontation is uncomfortable, you need to steel yourself for some constructive conflict. It will drain lots of your energy, but avoiding it will only make things worse.

Most importantly, take some time to recognize your own emotions about the client, the project, and the individuals involved. Self-knowledge can be key to your ability to diffuse the situation. If you are unaware of your own feelings about the situation, you are much more likely to be drawn into an unproductive conflict in the heat of the moment.

Once you have a handle on your feelings about the situation, you must make a conscious decision to set your emotions aside...for the moment. If you are to repair the relationship, you must be able to put the client's feelings ahead of your own.

3.1.2. Care

The final thing you have to do in preparation for healing client relationships is to care about your client. Genuinely care.

Caring about a client requires sensitizing yourself to their problems and concerns, caring about their professional and personal well-being, and committing yourself to the improvement of their condition.

Although we all like to think that we care all the time, it's very easy to slip. It's very easy to lie to ourselves about the level of commitment to a client.

Caring for a client is NOT:

- Wanting their business
- Enjoying your fees
- Liking the challenging work they bring you
- Priding yourself on their prestige

These are ways of fooling yourself into thinking that you're concerned about them when you're really concerned about you.

Some professionals are good actors and think that they can fake it. I don't believe it. Simulated caring is not enough. We are pack animals and at some level we can tell when someone's being disingenuous.   If you can't really care about a client, you may want to consider:

- Not working with them
- Referring them to another professional
- Reducing their dependence on you

Simulated caring is not enough.

Field Stories: Step 1

Throughout this chapter we will follow the stories of two professionals and their experiences of client conflict. In each Field Stories section, the left page will discuss the experiences of George, a project manager with a mid-sized IT consulting firm; the right page will cover Janice, an independent communications trainer and consultant. These stories are composites based on real-world experiences.

George is an experienced project manager currently working with two projects at different client sites. At United Technologies, he is leading a group of three programmers who are working to develop a set of custom financial reports for the Chief Financial Officer (CFO), Sandy.

Sandy has been with the company for eight years and has worked her way up the corporate ladder. Sandy reports to Roberto, the Chief Executive Officer who has been with the company for six months. He was brought in after the retirement of the charismatic founder of the firm.

The project has been underway for two months and is progressing well. Joe, the lead designer and programmer on the project has successfully guided it though half of the development of the software.

Janice is an independent trainer and consultant focusing on interpersonal communications. She has been out on her own for 10 years after being a sales person with a major candy manufacturer. She has developed her own custom courses that have been very well received at many large and small companies.

She has a two-year contract with Sanguinetec, a rapidly growing startup biotech company working to develop and market an artificial blood substitute. Each month she delivers her introductory communications class to all of Sanguinetec's new employees who have joined the company in the preceding month. Janice has delivered the monthly classes for 10 months.

The student review forms at the end of each class have showed strong appreciation for the content and delivery of the course.

Ed, the new Director of Human Resources, joined Sanguinetec six weeks ago after leaving a job in HR at a major defense contractor. He was induced to leave his old employer by the opportunity to manage a whole HR department, which he had never done before.

3.2. Step 2: Get the Facts

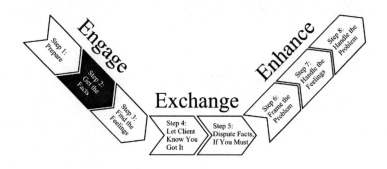

So you've prepared, but for what?

The second step in repairing the relationship is getting the facts of the situation on the table. What's important here is to understand the facts **AS THE CLIENT SEES THEM**. The purpose of this step is to get a clear picture of the client's beliefs about the situation: about what led up to and triggered the crisis.

Don't dispute the client's view of the world at this time. You may not agree that the client's facts are indeed facts. That's not important now. You're not trying to establish objective truth. You're just trying to learn what the client believes. There will be plenty of time later to come to agreement about what really happened and what it meant.

The key goal of this step is to understand, not to fix. If you don't understand what led to the breakdown in the relationship from the client's point of view, you have no hope of addressing the issue and saving the relationship. In other words, you can't fix what you don't see.

The key skill for success in this step is listening. You must be able to set aside your own feelings for the moment and listen to:

- What the client says
- What the client doesn't say
- What the client doesn't know how to say

Each will give you important insights into how to handle your situation.

3.2.1. Listen to What the Client Says

The first thing that you must listen for is what the client is actually saying. This will give you the first clues to the situation and triggers for your client's unhappiness. You will get a good picture of their immediate concerns and the level of urgency that they place on the problem.

Focus your best listening skills on the client. Hearing what other people say, really hearing them is very difficult. We spend most of our educational lives learning to think clearly and express ourselves articulately, but we are never taught to listen effectively.

Listening carefully to someone who is upset with you is especially difficult. It is a process with numerous barriers that you must be aware of and careful to avoid. Most of the time when others are talking we are:

- Daydreaming, not paying attention
- Thinking about what to say next
- Waiting to talk
- Filling in silently what we think that's being said
- Anticipating what we think is coming next

At this moment in the healing process, it is critical that you avoid these traps. You must focus on what the client tells you and then clarify it with them. To do this you should:

- Ask open-ended questions (ones that can't be answered yes/no)
- Listen to the responses
- Ask clarifying questions
- Paraphrase what was said to ensure that you got it.

3.2.2. Listen to What the Client Doesn't Say

Once you've clearly understood what the client has to say, keep listening. In fact, while you are listening to what they are saying, you also have the opportunity to listen to what they are NOT saying.

Although understanding what the client tells you is important, it may be more important to recognize what they are UNWILLING to tell you. Those hidden thoughts generally hold more power than those things that they will tell you. They are the ideas that they have thought about enough to make a conscious decision not to share.

Unspoken thoughts offer your best glimpse into the emotional content behind the unhappiness.

This may seem like an oxymoron. How can you listen to what's not said?

Easy. Listen for things like:

- Aborted sentences
- Long pauses
- Avoided subjects
- Unanswered questions

When any one of these things happens in the conversation, the client has probably decided to conceal something. At those times, you can often fill in the blanks and guess what's on their minds.

Making an educated guess about what's on the client's mind *after* listening to what the client says and doesn't say is not the same as making assumptions *before* listening. It's important to hear completely before adding your own interpretation.

The things clients won't tell you are often more important than the things that they will.

3.2.3. Listen to What the Client Doesn't Know How To Say

Finally, you need to listen for those things that the client doesn't know how to articulate. As with listening for what's not said, this too requires advanced listening skills. You must be able to analyze both what's said and what's not to determine whether something's missing. When they don't add up there is often some unspoken concern that lies at the heart of the matter.

Often, in the heat of confrontation, client complaints sometimes seem petty or small. They complain about things that ordinarily would be minor annoyances, yet the emotional force behind their concerns seems disproportionate to the magnitude of the complaint.

This is one key tip-off that the client is unable to translate real concerns into words - that whether or not they are willing to share their real issues, they cannot. The upsetting image is locked away, blocked either by emotion, lack of clarity, or inadequate words.

When you listen very carefully to the words that a client uses in describing the situation, they will give you clues to the hidden concern. The subtle shades of tone will guide you toward understanding the nature of the problem.

Field Stories: Step 2

At 2:30 on Friday afternoon, George picked up his voice mail messages and was disturbed to hear one from Sandy time stamped at 12:30. In a rather agitated voice she said, "George, where are you? I need to talk to you right away. I want Joe out of here and we need to have a replacement in by Monday morning."

George's first thought was that there was no one else available who could do the job. And even if there were, it would be a terrible idea to remove the only person with a complete technical understanding of the system midway through the project. But he knew that his facts would have to wait. First, he needed Sandy's facts.

George took a deep breath and dialed Sandy's number. "Sandy? George. I got your message. What happened?" "George, I've had it with Joe. I want him out of here today." "What happened?" "And I'm not going to pay for the last two weeks either." "Sandy, what happened?"

"This is the second Friday in a row that I can't find Joe. I didn't get my status report and have no idea how things are going." Sandy stopped. George waited silently until Sandy finally added, "I went to a meeting with Roberto and I got blindsided."

Janice was in her home office at 11:00 am on a Wednesday, enjoying a rare week without travel. She had spent a quiet morning catching up reading the backlog of journals and magazines piled up in her office. When the phone rang, she was startled by the sudden break in the silence. She hadn't spoken a word all day.

"Janice, this is Ed, the new HR Director at Sanguinetec, and I need to talk to you about the false charges on your most recent invoice."

Janice was quite taken aback. Not only had they never spoken before, but in ten years of consulting, no one had ever accused her of falsifying an invoice. She prided herself on her integrity and this sort of attack was like waving a red flag in front of a bull. She took a deep breath. She knew immediately what he was referring to. There was a special charge for a canceled class that she and Ed's predecessor had agreed to verbally. "Are you referring to the canceled class fee?" "Yes, and your contract states that there will be no cancellation fees. I don't work that way. Your services will no longer be required."

"Ed, I hope that you don't take this the wrong way, but I'm concerned that you haven't *asked* me why that's there. Would you like to know or do you just want to cancel the contract?"

3.3. Step 3: Find Feelings About the Situation

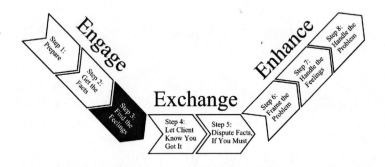

When a client complains to you, there are two distinct things that they are trying to communicate.

1. Their view of the facts surrounding and triggering their dissatisfaction.
2. Their feelings about those facts.

Only rarely will a client explicitly point out their emotions, but the whole reason that you're having the conversation is emotional. Dissatisfaction is an emotion, not a fact.

So just sticking to the facts is unlikely to heal the relationship. You need to deal with both the reasons and the reactions.

You can surface the feelings about the situation in several ways.

Watch and listen. The more emotionally charged the situation, the easier it will be to figure out. If the client's face is red, veins are bulging, and he is screaming at you, there's a good chance that he's angry.

Make a statement about the emotions, and then shut up. If given an opening, many clients will tell you what they are feeling. Give them the chance by saying something like, "You seem very frustrated." Then don't say anything. Allow the client to fill the silence. They will often tell you what's going on for them.

Ask. Although it feels odd to some people, you can ask what someone is feeling in a work setting. When a client gives you a fact about the problem, just ask, "How do you feel about that?" Often, they'll tell you.

All client conflict has its roots in emotions.

Field Stories: Step 3

George was starting to get the picture. Sandy was probably embarrassed and angry. George continued with questions. "What did Roberto hit you with?" "He wanted to make a decision about whether to expand the project to include another set of reports, but only if the current scope was under control. He had run into Joe in the hall a few days ago and got an update. He knew more about my project than I did!"

George waited a moment and then quietly said, "That must have been an embarrassing position to be in."

Sandy blurted out, "You bet it was. I felt like a total idiot. He probably thinks that I can't manage anything. And Roberto is still relatively new here. I can't afford that sort of exposure. I need someone in here who's going to help me, not someone who's going to make me look like a moron."

George asked, "Is there anything else here that I should know about?" Sandy paused and then added, "Even when he does give me information, it's usually not in a form that I understand. He doesn't understand what I need." George could feel the pent-up frustration and surmised that Joe's technical explanations probably made her feel incompetent.

Now Ed was taken aback. "Excuse me?" he managed to spit out.

"Ed, I'm not used to being accused of defrauding my clients and you are calling me with what seems like some awful assumptions about my ethics that you clearly have some strong feelings about."

"I've only been here six weeks and I've been finding contractors robbing this place blind everywhere I look."

"If that's true, I can understand your outrage, but I can't say that it feels fair to be presumed guilty and lumped in with a bunch of con artists. I imagine that you're probably under a lot of pressure to show quick results."

"My mandate is to transform this department into a professional HR organization within six months and I'm starting by tossing out the deadwood."

"Ed, It sounds like you've got a real challenge. It sounds intimidating, almost overwhelming. I'd like to sit down with you to share my observations of the department over the last year and to clear up this invoice issue. When can we get together?"

3.4. Step 4: Ensure The Client Knows You Got It

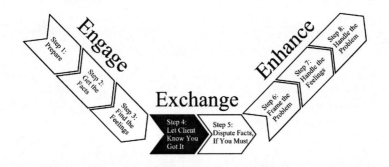

Now you begin to address the relationship problems. The other steps have laid the foundation for the resolution, but this is the turning point. Until this point you have been gathering information from the client without challenging, defending or questioning.

Once you have uncovered both the client's view of the facts of the situation and their feelings about it, it's time to make sure that the client understands that you've got it. This is critical because:

- It diffuses some of the emotion.
- It shows respect.
- It ensures that the client knows that you're both trying to solve the same problem.

You do this by:

- Summarizing what you've learned about the facts and emotions
- Asking the client if you've got it right

If the client says yes, then move on to the next steps.

If the client says no, or offers clarifications, go back to step 2, and continue doing this until the client agrees that you've got it right.

Once the client agrees that you understand their facts and feelings, you've created common ground. You now have created a common reality from which you can begin to heal the relationship.

Listening without confirmation is not much better than not listening.

Field Stories: Step 4

George felt that he had the information that he needed and that it was time that Sandy should know that he was listening.

"Sandy, I'd like to take a moment to recap to make sure that I've understood what's going on here. Is that OK with you?"

"OK, go ahead."

"I would appreciate it if you would stop me if I've got something wrong, because I want to be sure that I understand. What I heard was that you are feeling frustrated with Joe for two reasons, one immediate and the other longer term. The immediate reason is that you haven't been able to find Joe to get status updates on the last two Fridays and that led you to be embarrassingly blindsided in a meeting with Roberto. The longer-term frustration that I heard was that even when you do get information from Joe, it's not always in a form that makes sense to you. Would you say that that is an accurate summary of the situation?"

"Yeah. That's pretty much it."

"OK. Thanks. I think that I understand."

The following week, Janice and Ed met in his office at Sanguinetec.

Janice started out, "I appreciate your time and I hope that we can clear the air today. I'd like to talk to you about two things. I'd like to confirm what I have heard already and learn more about what I haven't yet heard. I'd like to start out making sure that I heard you clearly in our last conversation. Is that OK with you?"

"Go," Ed said succinctly.

"First, I understand that you have a concern over the validity of a class cancellation fee on my last invoice that was not specifically called out in our contract. Second, because of the charge, you would like to cancel our two-year contract. Correct?" "So far, you've got it right."

"I also heard that you've got a mandate to transform this department in six months and that you are starting out by eliminating questionable contractors." "Yup." "That's what I heard, but what I didn't hear was whether you have any other concerns about my services beyond the invoice. Are there any other problems?"

"Well, since you asked, I talked with two new employees, and neither liked your class much. I can't afford bad training."

3.5. Step 5: Question Facts…If You Must

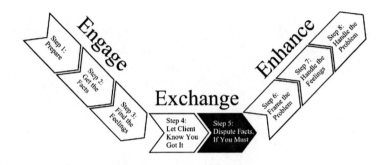

Now that you've gained agreement from the client that you've clearly heard their facts and feelings, you have a big decision to make: whether to dispute the client's version of the facts.

You cannot question a client's feelings. Their feelings are theirs and are not subject to question. Not only would that be pointless, it would be deeply disrespectful and insulting. Clearly it's not a productive thing to do.

You have, however, from listening carefully to the client, earned the right to question their version of the facts.

This is a very dangerous thing to do at this point. The relationship has only begun to heal and you may disrupt the progress by questioning the client's reality. Unless they have a VERY IMPORTANT fact wrong, it's probably not worth it.

If you disagree with the client's interpretation of the facts rather than the facts themselves, do not bring it up now. That's what the next step is for.

It can be very difficult to disagree with a client's fact and not to try to correct them. You must keep your need to be right under control. It will not serve your goal of retaining the client relationship.

If you must disagree, do so politely and carefully. It may be best to ask for time to investigate the situation, and then get back to the client shortly to continue the conversation.

Only question a client's version of the facts if you have a *very important* disagreement.

Field Stories: Step 5

"Sandy, I can understand your frustration, but there is one thing that I think we need to discuss. Last week, on Wednesday, you and I discussed briefly that I needed Joe for one day to help me out on another project. I know we didn't have an extended conversation about it, but I did clear it with you. That said, you still should have received a status update regardless of whether Joe was there on Friday or not. Do you remember our discussion about last Friday?"

"I suppose I do," Sandy said slowly. "But that doesn't change my mind about wanting Joe out of here."

"I understand. I just want to make sure that we're on the same page and that Joe isn't being blamed for more than he is actually responsible for. Does that seem fair to you?"

" I suppose so."

"Now, the reason you couldn't find Joe this morning is that he had a dentist appointment. He told me about it last week and I thought he had told you also. So on this, I have to apologize because it's my fault you didn't hear about it. I need to be clearer with Joe about sharing scheduling information with you as well as me."

Janice continued, "Anything else?" Ed answered, "No, that's it. That's why I want to cancel."

"Well, given the picture you must have of me and my services, I can understand your position. I'd like to start with the cancellation fee. This was a special one-time charge that your predecessor and I agreed to when he cancelled a class after I had already traveled to your Cambridge offices. He knew that he was going to cancel a week in advance and forgot to tell me. Not only did I incur all the travel expenses and lost time, but I also turned away another client for that week. We agreed that it would be fair that Sanguinetec at least pay for my travel expenses. That's what is contained in that charge. You can check with Connie in Cambridge if you'd like to confirm this."

"OK, I'm not sure that I agree with the decision, but I will live with it," Ed offered.

"I have also brought along the complete class review forms for all 10 of the classes that have been completed. Although the two people you talked to may not have been thrilled, I don't think that they represent a good sample. You'll find that the average scores are 4.5 out of 5 for student satisfaction."

3.6. Step 6: Frame the Problem

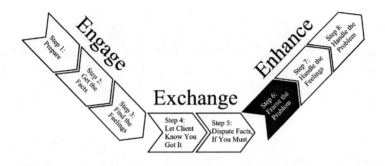

Once you and the client have agreed on the facts and feelings of the situation, it's time to jointly agree to the meaning. That meaning is the frame in which we place the facts. We often like to pretend that there is only one true interpretation of a set of facts, but it's not true.

Every set of facts can have multiple frames. For example, imagine that you and I are working together on a project and we agree that it is behind schedule. You may frame the situation such that it means that I am a slow worker. I may frame the situation such that we underestimated the effort required. Both of the meanings are validly constructed from the same facts.

In order to resolve the problem, you have to agree with the client what the actual problem is, and about how to frame the situation.

Since the client is upset, we can assume that the client has already framed the situation, and it is a frame that reflects poorly on the service provider.

Assuming that you want to continue to try to heal the relationship, you have two choices. You can accept the client's frame and offer restitution, or you can reframe the situation. There are times when it is appropriate to accept the client's interpretation, but most situations require reframing.

Proactively framing the situation requires taking much more control over the meaning of the situation than you have up to this time.

Should you decide not to reframe the situation, skip to the next step.

In order to resolve a problem, you have to agree with the client as to specifically what is the problem.

3.6.1. Identify Client Mental Model

The first step in reframing the situation is to identify the mental model that the client is currently applying to the situation.

A mental model is a simplified version of reality that we use to interpret a situation. Some models take the form of images or analogies that we use to reason about a situation. (E.g. this problem is like a boat going over a waterfall, and we're in the boat.) Other models take the form of rules and assumptions. (E.g. "If we encounter turbulence during our airplane flight, the plane might crash.")

So a client's mental model is a set of images, assumptions and/or rules that govern their thinking about the situation. You've already uncovered much of the information about their assumptions and about the facts and feelings that they have. Adding your observations about the language used to describe the situation will often give you a clear idea of the client's mental picture of the problem.

For example, imagine a situation in which a client is upset by being surprised that a project you are working together is late. They may have a mental picture of you deliberately hiding information from them in order to be self-serving and manipulative. You might figure this out from statements like, "Consultants always hide bad news."

Once you've figured out the mental model that the client is applying, you will also probably have a very good understanding of why they are upset.

A mental model is a simplified version of reality that we use to interpret a situation.

3.6.2. Create Your Own Mental Model

Now you must create your own model of the situation to replace the client's. Your model must not only be consistent with the facts that you've agreed to, but it also must be a more compelling interpretation of the facts than the one that the client has already adopted.

Finding an appropriate model is often a very intuitive exercise. However, here are two categories of models to help you generate ideas for your own interpretation.

Case-based models. Some models are built by extrapolating from one or more examples of situations. They are constructed by making inferences about general rules based on specific cases. These case-based models tend to be built on a limited number of experiences from which we infer general rules based on similarities of the cases. (E.g. Rule: Lawyers always charge more than they say they will. Cases: Both times I've gone to a lawyer, the bill has been higher in the end than the estimate at the beginning.)

Rule-based models. Rule-based models are exactly the opposite of case-based models. Rule-based models are based on abstract concepts, and then tested against specific cases to check whether the rules deduced hold against reality.

They can be deeply held beliefs that we are taught as children (e.g. Rule: If you put your elbows on the dinner table, you are being rude.) They can also reflect moral or ethical principles (E.g. Rule: Eating animals is wrong.)

You can use either to develop your mental picture of the client situation.

Defining the frame of a situation allows you to take control of its meaning and therefore its resolution.

3.6.3. Communicate the Model

No matter how compelling your alternative model of the situation is, if you do not communicate it to the client powerfully, you will be ineffective at changing the client's mental model. You must deliver the new interpretation in such a way that the client not only understands it, but also finds it convincing enough to abandon previously held ideas.

In their book, The Art of Framing, Gail Fairhurst and Robert Sarr identify five different ways to forcefully communicate mental models.

Metaphors efficiently deliver imagery and analogies. They are used to show how the current situation is like something else. (e.g. "We've been approaching this problem with a shotgun rather than a rifle.")

Jargon places a set of facts in familiar terms. It can create a set of strong associations with a very small amount of language.

Contrast shows how a situation is unlike another. It describes things by their opposites. Often it's easer to describe things by what they're not rather than by what they are.

Spin places a subject in a positive or negative context. Rather than reframe it, spin is used to create a judgment of the situation, effectively reframing.

Stories frame situations by example. They appeal especially well to people who tend to prefer the case-based models.

You need to select the approach to communicating the frame that will resonate best with this particular client.

If you cannot convince the client to accept your mental model, you cannot control the resolution of the situation.

Field Stories: Step 6

George realized that they had reached a critical point in the discussion. They had agreed on the facts of the situation and now had to come to agreement on the meaning of the facts. He also felt that he understood Sandy's mental model that was driving her unhappiness with Joe. She felt that Joe was both inattentive to her needs, and secretive about his work habits and the progress of the project, and that this sort of attitude would likely result in further problems as the project progressed.

George felt that the project itself was progressing well and that a change to the staffing of the project at this moment would jeopardize not only the project but also the customer relationship. Also, George realized that although he had addressed most of Sandy's factual complaints about Joe her emotions remained unchanged.

"Sandy, I think the failing in this situation has been mine and not Joe's. He's a young technical guy and I've been relying on him too much to keep you informed. He's been working very hard to keep this project on track and I think he's done a good job of it. From a technical standpoint the project is progressing well. Clearly, I need to do a better job of working with you. I think it would be a mistake to remove Joe now."

Ed agreed to look over the student reviews, but Janice felt that Ed still wasn't satisfied. Although he had not directly said so, she believed that Ed felt trapped by the long-term contract and that it prevented him from making visible changes to the department's projected image. Ed's mental model was that of a trapped animal looking for any way out of a cage. She might have blocked his immediate objections (escape attempt), but he wasn't done yet. Janice realized that she needed to change Ed's image of her from jailer to partner.

"Ed, I'm not in the business of trapping my clients. I'm in the business of helping them. We entered into a long-term arrangement to reserve dates and reduce costs. If after our discussion today you still want out, I'll be happy to discuss cancellation. But before we do that, I'd like to talk about how we can change what we do together to help your mission of transforming the department. Do you have a vision for the role you want training to play in the department?"

"Not specifically. I haven't had a chance to really dig into it. I've been so busy fighting fires and cleaning up messes."

"Do you have a plan for how you're going to develop that vision?"

"Not yet."

3.7. Step 7: Handle the Feelings About the Problem

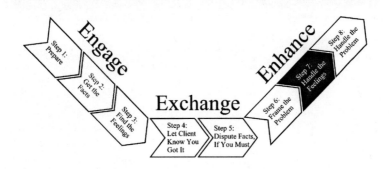

By this time, you and the client have built a consensus about the facts, feelings and frames of the situation. Finally, you are prepared to resolve the problem in a manner that will allow you to continue the relationship.

First you must handle the feelings about the problem. Handling feelings doesn't mean that you can fix them. You can only try to get past them.

There are several generic approaches to handling the client's feelings:

Empathize. Sometimes a little understanding is all that's required. There may be nothing specific that you can do about the client's hurt feelings other than to let them know that you understand how they feel. (E.g. "I understand how this must make you feel.")

Apologize. If it's appropriate, you may apologize for either the facts or the feelings. (E.g. "I'm very sorry that this happened." Or "Even though the problem was unavoidable, I'm very sorry for the stress that this has caused you.")

Ask what to do. Sometimes it's not really clear that there's anything concrete that you can do about the client's feelings. In those cases, it is sometimes best to ask the client something like, "What can I do to make this less painful for you?"

Be honest about your feelings related to the problem. If you have feelings about the situation that are appropriate to share, this is the time to do it. (E.g. "I'm so frustrated by this.")

Feelings are not a problem to be solved.

Field Stories: Step 7

George continued, "Don't punish Joe for my mistakes. I can't tell you how sorry I am to have caused you embarrassment in front of Roberto. I feel terrible about it. I'm sure you know that it was unintentional, but that probably doesn't make it any easier to accept. Is there anything I can do to help restore your relationship with Roberto?"

"No. I don't think there's any permanent damage, but I can't afford for that to happen again." Sandy seemed to be calming down a bit but was still clearly agitated.

" I understand. If you can accept my apology, I'd like to talk to you about what we can do together to ensure that this doesn't happen again."

"Well, what do you propose?"

"Ed, I can share with you what happened last time we tried to design a training program here. It turned out to be much more of a political minefield than we anticipated. The Operations and Research Department heads have very different ideas about what sort of training their people need. But, the CEO insists that we have the same program for everyone. If you would like, I can pull my notes and review them with you, and we can work together to design an approach to building a consensus with the department heads. Would that be helpful?"

"I suppose that it would. I hadn't really planned on involving them in the process until we had a training approach in place. Now that you mention it, your approach sounds less risky. What would it cost?"

"I don't know yet. I'll put together some options for you for the next time we meet. That way, you can choose how much or how little you would like me involved. Are you comfortable with that?"

"That sounds fine."

Janice sensed that Ed's stern mood was lightening a bit.

3.8. Step 8: Handle the Problems

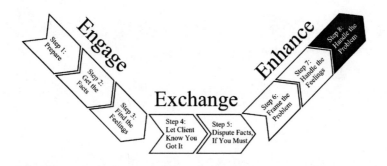

Finally, you are ready to deal with the substance of the problem.

This is the part that you as a professional have trained your whole career for. Most professional work is structured around finding problems and solving them through the application of the techniques of a specific discipline. Computer programmers write software to solve problems. Architects design buildings and spaces to solve problems and meet needs.

Based on the facts of the situation that you and the client have agreed to, you will construct an appropriate plan to restore the work or relationship to health.

Depending on the nature of the breakdown, there may be many remedies including financial exchanges, personnel changes, or unpaid work. There may be none.

Whatever you and the client agree to do together to restore the relationship to health, I recommend two specific things.

1. Document the agreement. Write a short letter reiterating the conversation, the facts and frame (and possibly the feelings), and the agreed resolution.

2. Follow through. No matter what you agree to, it is imperative that you follow through on your promises. If you do not, there is little hope of restoring the relationship.

If you follow these steps in order, you have a good chance of healing your client relationship.

Don't skip steps to get to Step 8 prematurely.

Field Stories: Step 8

"There are two things I can think of immediately that should help the situation. First, I need to get Joe a cell phone right away. That way even if he's not at his desk you should be able to find him more easily. Secondly, I'd like to schedule a regular weekly meeting with you so that the two of us can calibrate on the progress and problems related to the project in a more formal manner. After a few weeks I think we should review the frequency of this meeting so that we can strike a balance so that you are comfortable with the amount and timeliness of information but that I'm not wasting your time. I would hate for you to feel that you're not getting what you need. At the same time I'd hate for you to dread every time I walk into your office. How does that sound to you?"

"I think that would be a good start. We should try it out and see how it's going in a few weeks."

"Sandy, I appreciate your willingness to work with me on this. Again, I'm really sorry that this happened but I'm confident that within a few weeks you'll be comfortable with our progress. When would you like to schedule our first meeting?"

Janice noticed that their half hour was almost up. "I notice that we are almost at the end of our scheduled half hour and I don't want to put you off schedule, so I'd like to suggest that we return to the two immediate issues that brought us here. Are you comfortable with the one-time cancellation fee?"

"Yes, I understand it and will approve the bill for payment. But I don't want to continue with the classes that you have been teaching."

"That's fine. What I would like to suggest is that we put next month's class on hold and use the time for the strategic review that we will discuss at our next meeting. After that review, then we'll have a clearer idea of what sort of training would serve your needs."

"That sounds good. What would that mean for our costs?"

"That will depend on the options that you choose at our next meeting. Once you make that selection, we'll know whether we can continue to work together, or we will discuss cancellation. It'll be up to you. Sound fair?"

"Yes. I'm comfortable with that. Thanks for coming in, Janice."

4.What Not To Do

In this section, we discuss a number of common mistakes that prevent professionals from saving their client relationships.

While reading this section, look for your personal reactions to confrontations with clients. Try to be totally objective and honest with yourself. If you find that you have any of these habits, consider whether they will serve you well in your efforts to heal client relationships.

4.1. Get Defensive

Professionals are very protective and possessive about their work and relationships, which tends to put them on uncertain footing when confronted by a dissatisfied client. The natural reaction to an unhappy client is to feel attacked, and that often leads to defensive reactions.

Regardless of which stage of the process you are in when your defensive reaction occurs, it will stall or derail the process of relationship healing. In the early steps (1-3), the professional will begin to lose whatever trust has been restored through the conversation. In the later stages (5-8), the client will not be able to hear your attempts to solve the problem since they will be distracted by the defensive comments.

Defensive reactions to client complaints usually result in one of two things.

Transforming conversations into arguments. Most clients hear defensiveness as a denial of their concerns, and feel compelled to force the professional to understand and acknowledge their concerns. Both of you will tend to talk and neither listens. Clearly, this is not productive for moving through the healing steps.

Shutting down conversations altogether. Other clients hear defensiveness as a sign that it is pointless to continue the conversations with you at all. They are convinced that you are not listening and will abandon hope of restoring the relationship.

This doesn't mean that you cannot defend yourself in appropriate ways. But it must be done at the right time, and in the right way. Defense cannot be successfully mounted until at least step 5.

Defensiveness derails the healing process.

4.2. Counterattack

Counterattacks are just like defensiveness except that they dramatically increase the emotional content of the discussion. They have the same effects on the healing process as defensiveness except are even more destructive.

Counterattacks occur when, instead of trying to listen to client complaints or even defending yourself, you choose to attack the client instead.

If a client complains that a project is late, a counterattack might sound like: "You're not around enough to get timely feedback." Or, "Your managers are incapable of giving me the information I need." Or, "The family that owns the business is crazy. What would you expect?" However true the content of the attack may be, it is a diversion from the client's complaint, one likely to inflame rather than diminish the emotions of the situation and probably inspire counter-counterattacks from the client.

Counterattacks tend to happen when a professional is unprepared for a client complaint and that complaint is delivered forcefully. The high emotion of the complaint is met with equal emotion on the part of the professional.

As with defensiveness, attacks delay or derail the healing process. They are almost never productive.

4.3. Interrupt

When you were a little kid, your mother probably told you that it was rude to interrupt people. She was right. Some people like to delude themselves into thinking that it demonstrates how smart they are, or how in tune they are with the client's thinking. It doesn't.

In the context of healing client relationships, interrupting the client is rude and very disruptive to the healing process. It communicates indifference for the feelings of the client as well as disregard for the content of the message. Little could be more damaging to the healing process.

The goals of the first 4 steps of the process are to both learn about the client's perspective and to ensure that they know that you have heard it. Interrupting the client serves to undermine both goals.

Not interrupting can try your patience, especially when you feel that the client has the facts wrong.

Oddly enough, interrupting someone can come as a surprise to the interrupter. You may not consciously know that you're about to do it until it's too late. But there are ways to build your awareness of when you're about to jump in. There are two common clues that you might be preparing to interrupt. You might feel a strong urge to stop the other person from talking. You also might start formulating your response to something the client has said while the client is still talking. Once you notice either of these, stop yourself.

One of the few times that it may be acceptable, if unwise, to interrupt the client is to ask a clarifying question or to reflect what they have said to ensure that you understood.

4.4. Make Excuses

Yet another type of defensiveness is the excuse. Most of us have strong negative, childhood associations with excuses. We tried them out and they didn't work too well. "The dog ate my homework." Or the more recent Bart Simpson line "I didn't do it." Parents and teachers admonished us not to whine and make excuses for things that went wrong.

Those associations carry over into adulthood. When making excuses, professionals sound to clients like spoiled, whiny, over-paid children. Yes, this is judgmental on the part of clients; but, if you want to heal relationship problems, you'll just have to deal with it.

No matter how valid your excuses are, they tend to have the same effect on the healing process as other defensive responses. In steps 1-4, excuses tend to communicate two key things to the client that you'd probably rather they didn't think.

1. You're not listening to them.
2. You're more concerned about yourself than their problem and feelings.

In later stages of the process, you may be able to use the information as part of framing of the problem, but be very careful. These frames tend to sound too much like excuses and set off negative associations for the client.

- Uncontrollable circumstances
- Someone else's mistake
- Other urgent distractions (e.g. other clients)

When making excuses, professionals sound to clients like spoiled, whiny, over-paid children.

4.5. Jump to a Solution

Most professionals are well trained in the art of problem solving. Their entire work life is spent in the resolution of client problems, and they are eager to apply those skills. Especially when faced with an unhappy client, the pressure to solve the problem is enormous.

Unfortunately, sometimes professionals feel so much pressure that they want to jump directly to the solution. In the relationship healing process, that would mean skipping one or more of steps 2-7, which usually won't work. By skipping steps, you fail to gather the information that you need to solve the problem and the client is deprived of the emotional healing that the process provides. On rare occasions, it may also leave you open to being duped.

I used to have a client who was a master at taking advantage of this phenomenon. I had an office right next to his, so I got to watch him at work. He liked to call a service provider into his office, shut the door, and complain. These were not gently delivered, well thought out concerns. He would yell and scream for 20 minutes at a time using profanity that I never learned growing up on the south side of Chicago. His insult-laced tantrums generally didn't contain much useful information for the consultant. But by the time the screaming stopped, the consultant wasn't eager to ask any questions for fear that another tirade would start. The consultant would just skip right to step 8, trying to handling the problem without really knowing what was wrong. He would usually offer free service, rebates or some other costly remedy. The client would think about it for a few minutes, and then accept and walk out of his office with a self-satisfied smirk on his face.

Those lcaps to solutions cost the consultant dearly.

Most of the time, when you jump to a solution, you are trying to solve the wrong problem. Normally, this will tell the client you're not listening. Occasionally, it may lead to being taken advantage of.

4.6. Assume That You Know the Problem

Although the relationship healing process recommends always being prepared for a client to complain, you can be too prepared. When you're concerned about some aspect of a project and the client calls to complain, there's a tendency to assume that the client is going to complain about whatever you were worried about before the call.

This type of situation is commonly portrayed in television sitcom shows. A guy sneaks out on a date when his girlfriend isn't around and when she calls the next morning upset about something minor and completely unrelated, he assumes that she caught him and he confesses. It's usually only a few seconds before the conflict escalates.

The reason that you can see this story line almost every night of the week is that we really do that. It's funny because we recognize the situation and empathize with the characters.

In our professional life, it's just as bad. You might end up confessing to something that the client didn't call to complain about. You might escalate the problem beyond what it was.

More commonly and less amusingly, when you correctly anticipate what the client is going to complain about, you interrupt the relationship healing process. You prevent them expressing themselves and having both the satisfaction of speaking and of being heard.

Make sure you really know what the client is upset about.

4.7. Believe Delivery is Enough

If you look at the list in section 2.1 about what clients want, you'll notice that relatively few of the items are directly related to delivery of the service. Most of them are related to the *way* that the service is delivered, not the quality of the service.

Why? Because clients judge the quality of a service based on those other factors. Why not judge the quality of the service directly? Because they can't. They hire you because you are a specialist in something that they don't understand completely enough to resolve their own problems. Judging the quality of the service would require specialist knowledge that they don't possess. If they knew enough to judge directly, they wouldn't need you. Therefore they judge based on proxies.

One of the most common mistakes that professionals make is failing to understand this. They think that clients only want them to deliver brilliant services and end up ruining the client relationship in the process.

In the relationship healing model, this leads to skipping steps 3 and 7, finding the feelings and handling the feelings. You may be very capable of resolving the service problem that triggered the relationship crisis, but if you don't recognize and handle the feelings associated with the problem, the relationship won't heal. The raw emotions will remain an open wound that will eventually undermine the client relationship.

Clients judge the quality of your service by their experience, not your product.

4.8. Focus on Yourself

Another common mistake is to focus inward when the crisis occurs. It's natural when you're feeling under attack to pull back and think about yourself, but you've got to fight that urge.

Successfully repairing client relationships requires first focusing completely on the client, then integrating your self-interest later.

Notice that steps 2-4 of the process are completely client focused. If in those early stages you start to turn inward, it will become apparent to the client and the process will break down.

Many of the pitfalls listed in this section are forms of focusing on you rather than on the client. Doing so will lead to skipping steps in the relationship healing process or in following them disingenuously. Either way, the relationship is unlikely to improve.

4.9. Try to Look Smart

Most professionals are smart - very smart. They are highly educated and articulate. They often make the mistake of trying too hard to show it in order to make a good impression on the client.

This can be disastrous during client conflict. It's generally unwise at any time, but is particularly distracting when trying to heal a relationship. It will appear to the client that you are too focused on yourself and your image and not enough on them and their problem.

Types of behavior that fall under the try-to-look-smart category include:

Using impenetrable jargon. When you start trying to explain things using technical language that the client doesn't understand, they assume that you are either being condescending or obfuscating. Neither of these will give the client a good impression.

Qualifying client statements. When a client is in the midst of telling you something about their problem, resist the urge to try to refine their statements unless the qualification is important to the conversation. If the client says something like "The software doesn't work when the moon is full," don't add, "Only when it falls on a

Tuesday." You sound like a "know-it-all" and that's not what the client needs during a conflict.

Contradicting minor facts. Just as a client doesn't need to have their statements "improved" with irrelevant qualifications, they don't need to have minor details corrected either. When the client complains "One of your staff has been out every Friday for a month," don't tell them "Actually, he made it here once."

Appearing pompous or condescending does not inspire confidence.

4.10. Try to Force Premature Closure

As you go through the healing process with your client, there will be a moment at which you first grasp how the problem can be resolved. You will have a flash of insight about what happened, and what will satisfy the client. You will feel a combination of elation, relief and excitement. You will see the light at the end of the long dark corridor.

That is *not* the moment to tell the client about your revelation.

Don't let that enthusiasm out. Chances are that the client isn't ready to settle the matter yet. The client needs to complete the emotional cycle before being ready for a solution.

This is especially important for professionals who are uncomfortable with conflict. Don't let *your* discomfort drive you when you try to get the client to agree to a resolution. You must let *their* readiness drive the timing of when you suggest a resolution and when you push for closure.

When you do make an offer to resolve the problem, do not expect that your client will have the same enthusiasm for the resolution that you do. It will take time for the client to gain comfort with resolving their concerns and the specific measures you recommend.

Expect that it will take the client a bit of time to accept what you have offered. Allow that time. If you try to pressure the client to take an offer, you may solve the problem but undermine the healing of the feelings, damaging the healing process.

4.11.   Avoid Conflict

The relationship healing process is designed to channel conflict into productive discussion, not to avoid conflict or prevent it.   Constructive conflict tends to occur anywhere from steps 5 through 8. After you have listened to the client, understood their concerns and feelings, and made sure that they know that you got it, you have earned the right to initiate constructive conflict.

Avoiding conflict will prevent you from resolving the problem and healing the relationship. It has often been said that good relationships are not based on an absence of conflict, just on constructive conflict.   It's   true.   For disagreements to be settled and issues worked out, conflict is sometimes necessary. Avoiding conflict won't make it go away, it will only make things worse.

To ensure that things stay constructive:

Stay on topic. Bringing in other subjects and complaints during a conflict only dilutes focus and irritates your client. Save other things for another time.

Don't get personal. Stick to the problem, not the person. When things get personal, you crank up the emotion and lose perspective, exactly the opposite of what you want to achieve.

Don't generalize. If you've got to raise an issue, don't be vague. Your client needs to know exactly what's bothering you. You can also slip into exaggeration that will be unproductive.

Avoid false agreement. Don't agree with something just to be agreeable. If something is important, explore it.

Don't repeat. You don't reach resolution by just repeating the same argument over and over. It's just annoying.

4.12. Avoid Eye Contact

The healing process is designed to help restore trust to your client relationship. You don't want to do anything to undermine that trust.

Many studies have been done to try to identify how information is communicated between people. Most of the studies have found that information is communicated three ways:

1. Body Language
2. Tone of Voice
3. Words

Professionals focus mostly on communicating through words and their meanings. Unfortunately, they have been found to be the least effective channel for communication. Your client will learn much more about your sincerity in resolving the conflict from your tone of voice and body language.

In American culture, one of the most important components of body language is direct eye contact. It is taken as a sign of honesty. Avoiding eye contact carries strong negative messages that you cannot afford to send. Although some people are less comfortable than others in looking into another person's eyes, in this case it is very important to try.

If a client feels you are avoiding eye contact, they will wonder what you are trying to hide.

Words are the least effective form of interpersonal communication.

4.13.   Mismatch Client Urgency

Because there are usually strong feelings involved when client conflict occurs, it's important to take note of a client's sense of urgency about a problem and to properly mirror it. If you don't properly match the client's sense of urgency, it makes relationship healing much more difficult if not impossible.

If the client feels a higher sense of urgency than you reflect, then they perceive your response as inadequate. They feel that you don't understand the importance of the problems or their feelings about the problems. As a result, the client feels that your response is dismissive, inadequate or belittling.

If you show a higher sense of urgency than the client, then the client will be uneasy, wondering whether you are hiding something more important or know something that they don't.

Either way, trust building has been interrupted and relationship healing diminished.

You have several tools that you can use to help you reflect the appropriate level of urgency.

Speech pattern. You can use your voice to indicate urgency. By varying the speed, volume and tone of your voice, you can reflect many different levels of importance.

Timing of response. You reflect the importance of a problem by how long you take to get back to a client. If you don't respond to their initial calls for days, it's quite different than responding within five minutes.

Statements. You can also make direct statements to the client like, "I understand how urgent it is that we address this issue."

5.Preventing Client Conflict

The best way to heal client relationships is to avoid damaging them altogether. Although no complex, long-term relationship will ever be completely without problems, there are some simple preemptive steps that you can take to minimize conflict.

5.1. Calibrate Regularly

The longer you go without calibrating with your client, the more likely relationship problems are to arise. Clients most often complain about professionals not meeting their expectations. If you don't regularly discuss those expectations, you're asking for a mismatch to crop up and the relationship to falter.

A common mistake is to confuse regular contact with a client with calibration. Just because you have seen a client, or even discussed specific issues relating to work, it does not mean that you have effectively calibrated.

Client calibration includes explicit discussion about:

Progress of project. Discuss what's been completed, what hasn't, what's planned for completion and when, and what known obstacles exist.

Feelings about progress and process. Assess and discuss the client's comfort and feelings about both the progress of the project and the process that it's following.

Expectations about project, process and feelings. Ask specifically whether the project is meeting their expectations and what expectations they have for the future.

Internal events.   Discuss events in the organization and project that may affect success.

External events.   Discuss events outside the immediate organization that affect success.

Regular calibration will minimize problems and reduce their intensity should they occur.

5.2. Don't Accept Impossible Assignments

Many client relationships fail because of projects that never should have been started in the first place. Many projects fail to meet client expectations because they started with difficult or impossible goals to meet.

In a rush to secure business, you can be overly optimistic about how achievable a project goal may be. You may delude yourself about how realistic a project is. You may fall under the spell of a client's charismatic enthusiasm. You may know that it's impossible, but think that you can manage the client's expectations once the project is underway.

This is a serious breech of professionalism. Clients need and deserve the candor and perspective of outside professionals. They may want yes people, but they've probably already got lots of them around. They pay your fee to tell them when they've got a bad idea.

Accepting impossible projects is also a very bad business practice. In addition to being unethical, it nearly ensures that the client relationship is doomed. You will not only lose the fee, you might get sued or lose your reputation in the community.

5.3. Follow Your Instincts

"Trust the force, Luke," Obi-Wan Kenobi urges at the end of the first Star Wars movie. Here I make the same recommendation. You can foresee many relationship problems, if you only trust your instincts.

Many client relationship problems are apparent from the beginning. You leave that first client meeting with a vague uneasiness. You watch while the client berates a subordinate in a public meeting. You listen while the client cusses out a vendor. You notice that everyone in the office seems to be walking on eggshells.

There are many things that can tip you off that something about this relationship will be difficult to manage. But, in a rush to get the business, you shake it off.

Don't.

Many times, those vague feelings of unease are valid warnings of problems to come. Pay attention to them.

If you feel uneasy about a project or a client, examine it closely before dismissing it. You probably wouldn't throw away any other tool in your customer service bag. Why would you abandon this one? If you can't specifically identify what's wrong, don't just ignore it. Examine it.

Pay attention to your instincts. They're usually right.

5.4. Close When You're Done

If you have given a client all the high value services that you can, there's only one thing to do. Leave. Not only is it the ethical thing to do, it's also good for your relationship. Hanging around and providing low value services leaves you very vulnerable to client conflict.

When clients feel that you're working on things of great value to them, they have a high tolerance for mistakes, problems, and small insults. When they feel that you're only working on things of small value, they are much more likely to complain about even the smallest concern.

Imagine that you're about to have open-heart surgery. Your doctor has referred you to someone he believes is the best surgeon within 500 miles. You go to the office for your initial consultation and you're forced to wait 90 minutes to see him. You'd probably be a little upset, but would you complain? Probably not. He's the best and you only want your life in the hands of the best.

Now imagine that you need a haircut and a friend has referred you to her stylist. You go for your appointment and have to wait 90 minutes to get your hair cut. Would you complain? Probably. Our tolerance for inconvenience is proportionate to the importance and scarcity of the service we seek.

If you stick around with a client when you don't have high value to add, you are likely to have a contentious relationship. When you're done providing high value service, leave. If they perceive that you've delivered good value, they'll call back.

5.5. Challenge Mistaken Expectations

Clients rarely establish business relationships with professionals to do things that they consider unimportant. Hiring a professional represents a substantial risk to a client. They are paying for a service that will have undetermined effects on their businesses. Even worse, a professional's work may damage the client's career and business.

They pay our high fees only because they have high expectations for the value that we deliver and these expectations, in turn, govern the trajectory of the relationship.

Because of all the risks involved in hiring a professional, clients often have difficulty deciding to approve a first assignment. But if they have extremely high expectations for the value of that assignment, they are more likely to approve it. Of course, the higher the expectations, the more likely they are not to be met, resulting in client conflict. So the same expectations that make an assignment likely to happen make it likely to crash and burn.

The only way to avoid this problem is to constantly monitor a client's expectations for the results of your work, and correct mistakes as soon as you recognize them. If a client believes that some unlikely benefit will accrue due to your work, you have an obligation to correct that impression as soon as possible.

Although it may be tempting to allow excessive expectations to drive a sales cycle to closure, it is a strategy that ensures a difficult relationship later by undermining the trust upon which professional relationships must be based.

Allowing unrealistic expectations to go unchallenged is unethical, unprofessional, and unprofitable.

5.6. Don't Play Internal Politics

Another way to wind up with unhappy clients is to take part in their internal politics.

As an external service provider, you play an unusual role within client organizations. You are not a member of the company, yet you are privy to many of the organization's most important decisions and political processes.

First we need to be clear about office politics. There are two types of politics.

Self-serving politics. When you mention business politics to most people, they immediately think about the petty bickering and power grabbing that is all too common in the workplace. That's a subset of politics called self-serving politics. Whenever the conversation about a decision is based on "what's mine" rather than "what's right for the organization" then there's self-serving politics going on.

Positive politics. Whenever an organization needs to make a decision and no immediate consensus forms, a political process ensues. Positive politics is an organization's way of making decisions about what's best for the group.

As a professional, most of your work with clients will involve significant decisions for their businesses. As such, you must participate in their political processes...but very carefully.

In addition to being unprofessional, allowing yourself to be drawn into an individual's self-serving political processes will frequently lead to conflict with one client faction or another. It may lead to more business in the short term, but eventually, it will turn out badly.

5.7. Refuse Assignments Without Goals

Clients often know what they want you to do, even if they don't know what they want you to achieve. You can recognize this because a client tells you something like, "I want you to write my Will." Or, "I want you to teach a training class on project management." Or, "I want you to program my computer to deliver these six reports." In these cases, the client has told you what activities they want performed, not what goal they want to fulfill.

You can recognize situations like this rather easily. All you need to ask are three questions about the client's request.

1. What does the client want me to do?
2. How does the client want me to do it?
3. Why does the client want this?

Usually the client will answer #1, may have an opinion about #2, and says little to nothing about #3. The answer to #3 is the most important. It's the goal of the assignment.

If you are bidding on a job without getting a very clear answer to #3, you are doing both you and your client a disservice. Often when a client asks for a task to be performed, they are assuming that it will fill some unstated need.

You, as a professional, have an obligation to determine whether that is true. Since you are the expert, generally you are much better able to assess whether the task fits the goal. If you do not ask, you are set to disappoint the client. You may perform the task perfectly, but if it doesn't produce the client's desired result, relationship problems will ensue.

Also, if you do not know the goals of a service, you don't know the value to the client, and can't avoid the low value/low tolerance trap.

6. Building Professional Skills

6.1. Developing Client Management Skills

The life of a professional is not an easy one. You spend most of your educational years learning the skills of your trade, learning how to deliver your services. Most then move on to join a professional service firm or become employees of large companies where early careers focus on the detailed application of those skills learned in school. You work day and night cranking out software, writing briefs, or performing audits. Grunt work.

Only later do you learn that there is much more to the profession than you learned in school. Delivery of the service is only the starting point. Those skills that you struggled to acquire are just the minimum necessary to get in the door of the field.

Whether you are a young professional or a seasoned veteran, as long as you stay in your chosen field, you will constantly work to expand your knowledge and skills. That's both the joy and the bane of being a professional.

Congratulations. By reading this book and others like it, you are taking another step toward expanding your vision of your field. I will not pretend that any one book, seminar, or lecture will completely transform your career. Each one has its place in the journey. I hope that you have found this one useful and will choose to go out into the world and apply these techniques.

Now it's up to you. Only through practice and courage can you develop and improve your abilities in:

- Establishing client relationships
- Managing client relationships
- Healing client relationships
- Selling follow-on work

Resources

Burley-Allen, Madelyn. <u>Listening: The Forgotten Skill</u>. John Wiley & Sons, 1995.

Fairhurst, Gail T., and Sarr, Robert A. The Art of Framing. Jossey-Bass, 1996.

Beckwith, Harry. Selling the Invisible: A Field Guide to Modern Marketing. Warner Books, 1997.

Maister, David, Green, Charles, and Galford, Robert. The Trusted Advisor. Free Press, 2000.

About the Author

Paul Glen is a management consultant, professional speaker, trainer, and educator. He founded C2 Consulting and the Technical Consulting Skills Institute (TCSI) to help advance the management of IT organizations and projects.

Mr. Glen is a part-time faculty member in the MBA program at the University of Southern California's Marshall School of Business where he teaches a second year elective course that he designed on e-Business Strategy. He has also taught in the MBA program at Loyola Marymount University.

Mr. Glen received his MBA from the J. L. Kellogg Graduate School of Management at Northwestern University with majors in marketing, organizational behavior, and strategy. He received a BA from Cornell University with majors in computer science and mathematics.

Mr. Glen has more than a dozen years of experience delivering and managing IT related products and services. Before founding C2 and TCSI, he was Western Regional Manager for SEI Information Technology, a national IT consultancy.

Mr. Glen is a Professional Member of the National Speakers Association and is affiliated with the Institute of Management Consultants, the American Society for Training and Development, the Academy of Management, and the Professional Coaches and Mentors Association.

Index

PROFESSIONAL SERVICE
PUBLISHING

PROFESSIONAL SERVICE
PUBLISHING

Order Form

🖨 **Fax Orders**: 310-574-1061 Fax this form.

☎ **Telephone Orders**: Call 877-814-7753 toll free. Have your credit card ready.

🖳 **Web Orders:** www.c2-consulting.com

📠 **Email Orders**: orders@c2-consulting.com

✉ **Postal Orders**: Orders, Professional Service Publishing, 17 Northstar Street, Suite 202, Marina Del Rey, CA 90292

Please send me:

Copies	Item
_____	Healing Client Relationships Book
_____	Healing Client Relationships Audio CD Set

Please send FREE information on:

❑ Other Books   ❑ Speaking

❑ Consulting   ❑ Seminars

❑ Customized Books   ❑ Newsletter

Volume Book Pricing	
# Copies	Discount
25-99	20%
100-499	30%
500-999	40%
1,000 & up	50%

Name: _____

Address: _____

City: _____ State: _____ Zip: _____

Country: _____ Telephone: _____

Email: _____

Sales Tax: Please add 8% sales tax for orders shipped to California addresses.

Shipping: US: $4 for first item, $2 for each additional. International: $9 for first item, $5 for each additional (est.)

Payment: ❑ Visa ❑ MasterCard ❑ Amex ❑ Discover

Number: _____ Exp: ____ / ____

Name on Card: _____

PROFESSIONAL SERVICE
PUBLISHING

PROFESSIONAL SERVICE
PUBLISHING

Order Form

🖨 **Fax Orders**: 310-574-1061 Fax this form.

☎ **Telephone Orders**: Call 877-814-7753 toll free. Have your credit card ready.

💻 **Web Orders:** www.c2-consulting.com

📧 **Email Orders**: orders@c2-consulting.com

✉ **Postal Orders**: Orders, Professional Service Publishing, 17 Northstar Street, Suite 202, Marina Del Rey, CA 90292

Please send me:

Copies	Item
_____	Healing Client Relationships Book
_____	Healing Client Relationships Audio CD Set

Please send FREE information on:

❏ Other Books   ❏ Speaking

❏ Consulting   ❏ Seminars

❏ Customized Books   ❏ Newsletter

Volume Book Pricing	
# Copies	Discount
25-101	20%
100-500	30%
500-1000	40%
1,000 & up	50%

Name: _____

Address: _____

City: _____ State: _____ Zip: _____

Country: _____ Telephone: _____

Email: _____

Sales Tax: Please add 8% sales tax for orders shipped to California addresses.

Shipping: US: $4 for first item, $2 for each additional. International: $9 for first item, $5 for each additional (est.)

Payment: ❏ Visa ❏ MasterCard ❏ Amex ❏ Discover

Number: _____ Exp: ____ /_____

Name on Card: _____